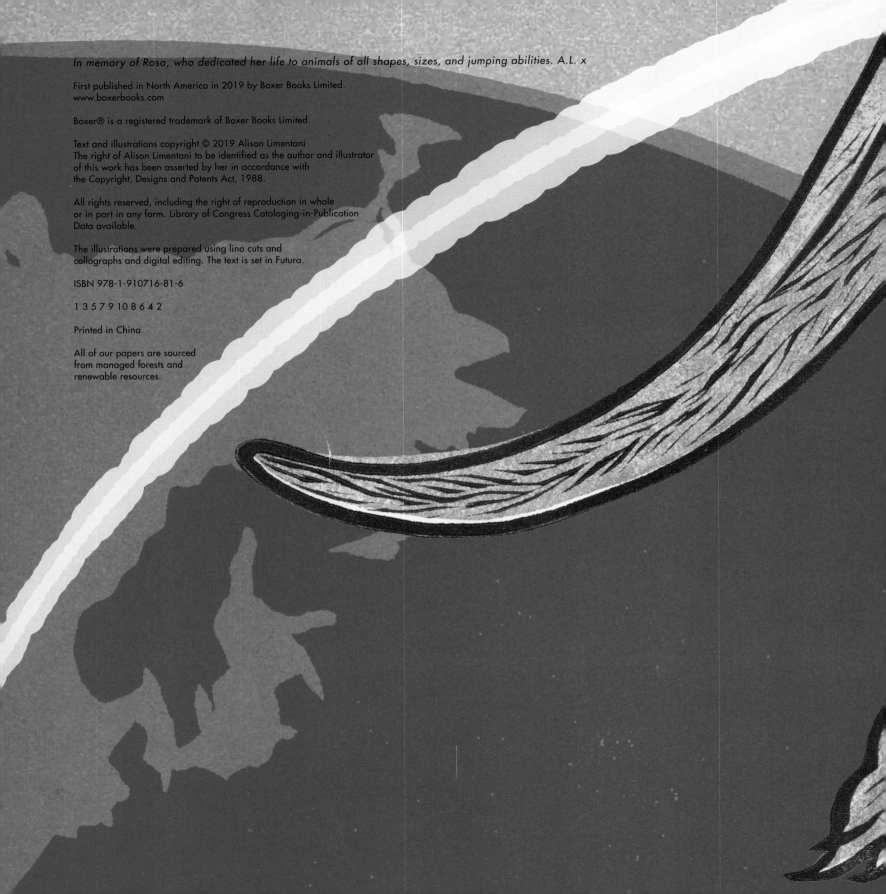

First published in North America in 2019 by Boxer Books Limited.
www.boxerbooks.com

Boxer® is a registered trademark of Boxer Books Limited.

The illustrations were prepared using lino cuts and
collographs and digital editing. The text is set in Futura.

ISBN 978-1-910716-81-6

1 3 5 7 9 10 8 6 4 2

Printed in China

All of our papers are sourced
from managed forests and
renewable resources.

HOW FAR CAN A KANGAROO JUMP?

ALISON LIMENTANI

Boxer Books

1 kangaroo jump is 30 feet,

which is further than the Olympic world record for long jumping,

and the same distance as

2 ring-tailed lemur leaps,

which is the same
distance as

3 penguin porpoises,

which is the same
distance as

4 rabbit hops,

which is the same distance as

5 tree frog bounces,

which is the same distance as

6 goat skips,

which is the same
distance as

7 cassowary bounds,

which is the same distance as

8 coyote vaults,

which is the same distance as

9 grasshopper hurdles,

which is the same distance as

10 chipmunk springs,

which is not nearly
as far as . . .

1 snow leopard pounce,

which is nearly twice as far as a kangaroo jump!

But how many kangaroo jumps would it take to get all the way around the earth?

4.4 million jumps,

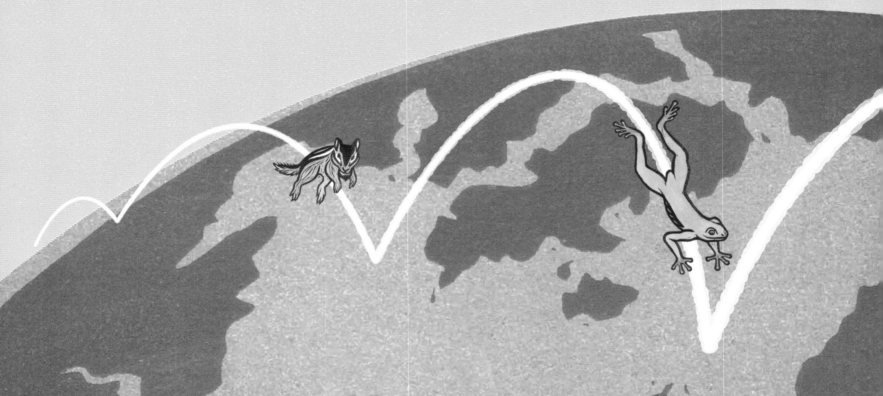

or 22 million tree frog bounces, or 44 million chipmunk springs,

or 2.6 million snow leopard pounces! How far can **YOU** jump?

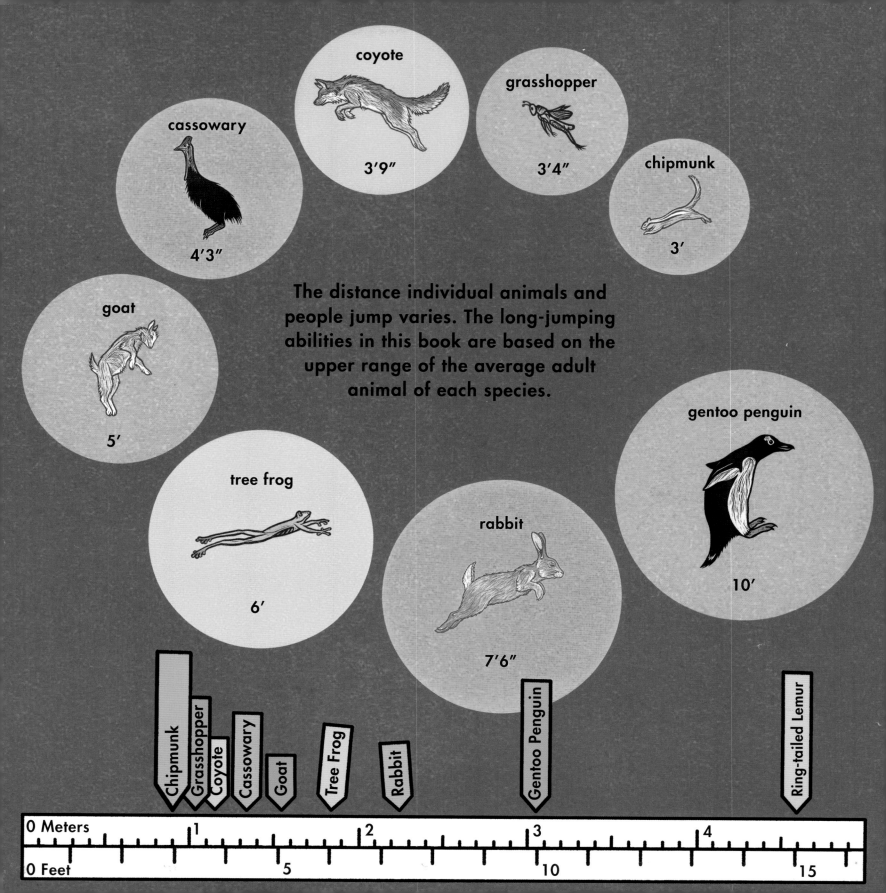

coyote

cassowary

grasshopper

chipmunk

3'9"

3'4"

3'

4'3"

goat

The distance individual animals and people jump varies. The long-jumping abilities in this book are based on the upper range of the average adult animal of each species.

gentoo penguin

5'

tree frog

rabbit

6'

7'6"

10'

Chipmunk

Grasshopper

Coyote

Cassowary

Goat

Tree Frog

Rabbit

Gentoo Penguin

Ring-tailed Lemur

0 Meters | 1 | 2 | 3 | 4

0 Feet | 5 | 10 | 15